PEOPLE
FACTS.

BY
FRANZISKA LIEBIG & JULIAN REALE

BIS Publishers
Borneostraat 80-A
1094 CP Amsterdam
The Netherlands
T +31 (0)20 515 02 30
bis@bispublishers.com
www.bispublishers.com

ISBN 978 90 6369 623 8

Copyright © 2021 Franziska Liebig, Julian Reale and BIS Publishers.

Edited by Zulfikar Abbany.

Art direction and illlustrations by Franziska Liebig.

www.people-facts.com

DID YOU KNOW THAT HALLUCINATORY VOICES SOUND DIFFERENT IN DIFFERENT
COUNTRIES, AND THAT THEY ARE INFLUENCED BY LOCAL CULTURE?
DID YOU KNOW THAT TEARS SHED IN SADNESS ARE DIFFERENT FROM TEARS
SHED IN JOY?

WELL, NEITHER DID WE. SO, WE DECIDED TO COLLECT THE MOST BIZARRE AND
AMAZING FACTS WE COULD FIND ABOUT PEOPLE AND LIFE AND PUT THEM ALL IN
THIS BEAUTIFULLY ILLUSTRATED BOOK. WE CALL IT PEOPLE FACTS.

TO MAKE IT EASIER FOR YOU TO NAVIGATE THIS WEIRD WORLD OF OURS,
WE'VE ORGANISED OUR EXPLORATION IN THE CATEGORIES:

BODY FACTS
MENTAL FACTS
MOTHER NATURE FACTS
CULTURAL FACTS

EVERY SINGLE FACT IS BACKED UP BY SCIENCE, SO YOU CAN
LOOK UP THE SOURCES IN THE APPENDIX.

HAVE FUN AND ENJOY!

BODY
FACTS.

IT IS POSSIBLE FOR TWINS TO HAVE DIFFERENT FATHERS.

MOST PEOPLE ONLY EVER USE ONE NOSTRIL WHEN THEY BREATHE
THROUGH THE NOSE. BUT THE TWO NOSTRILS ALTERNATE REGULARLY.

BOTOX MAKES IT HARDER FOR PEOPLE TO COMMUNICATE.

IT'S A SUBSTANCE USED IN MEDICINE AND COSMETICS, BUT IT MAY AFFECT YOUR ABILITY TO INITIATE FACIAL EXPRESSIONS IN FACE—TO—FACE CONVERSATIONS. WE ALSO UNCONSCIOUSLY COPY EACH OTHER'S FACIAL EXPRESSIONS TO SHOW WE'RE ENGAGED IN THE CONVERSATION, IT CREATES A SHARED UNDERSTANDING.

BUT A FACE THAT'S BEEN TREATED WITH BOTOX IS LESS ABLE TO MOVE NATURALLY AND THAT CAN CREATE THE IMPRESSION THAT YOU'RE LESS INVOLVED OR INTERESTED. PEOPLE WILL PICK UP ON THAT.

TEETH ARE YOUR ONLY BODY PARTS THAT CANNOT HEAL THEMSELVES.

THE HUMAN EYE HAS THE
EQUIVALENT OF 576 MEGAPIXELS.

WHEN OBSERVED UNDER A MICROSCOPE, YOUR TEARS CAN REVEAL
WHY YOU CRIED. TEARS SHED IN SADNESS LOOK DIFFERENT
FROM THOSE SHED IN JOY, AND DIFFERENT AGAIN FROM THOSE YOU
CRIED WHILE CUTTING ONIONS.

BRAIN DAMAGE CAN MAKE YOU LOSE THE ABILITY TO SPEAK. BUT SOME PEOPLE MAINTAIN THE ABILITY TO SWEAR. THAT MAY BE BECAUSE CURSING IS ANCHORED DEEPER IN THE BRAIN REGION THAT'S PREDOMINANTLY RESPONSIBLE FOR LANGUAGE.

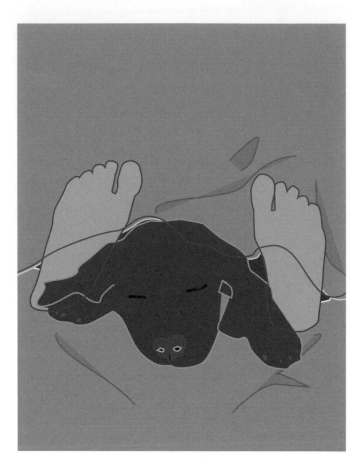

THERE ARE JUST TWO ANIMALS THAT SLEEP ON THEIR BACKS:
HUMANS AND GIANT KANGAROOS.

SMILING FOR NO REASON WILL MAKE YOU HAPPIER.

AND KEEPING AN UPRIGHT POSTURE WILL MAKE YOU FEEL MORE CONFIDENT. WE CAN INFLUENCE OUR STATES OF MIND WITH GOOD POSTURE AND GOOD GESTURES. IT'S SAID THAT PHYSICAL GESTURES GENERATE REAL FEELINGS.

WHAT DO SEX ADDICTS AND DRUG ADDICTS HAVE IN COMMON? ORGASMS AND SOME DRUGS, LIKE HEROIN, STIMULATE HEIGHTENED ACTIVITY IN THE SAME BRAIN REGIONS.

HUNGER MAKES PEOPLE UNBEARABLE.

IT CAN MAKE US AGGRESSIVE. BUT IT'S PRECISELY THAT IMPULSE THAT SPURS US TO HUNT FOR FOOD.

ASTRONAUTS GROW IN SPACE.

BOTOX AS AN ANTIDEPRESSANT?

A META STUDY OF SAFETY SURVEILLANCE DATA HAS SUGGESTED THAT BOTOX COULD BE USED TO TREAT PEOPLE SUFFERING WITH SOME FORMS OF DEPRESSION. WHEN INJECTED IN THE FOREHEAD, WHERE PEOPLE FROWN, PEOPLE WERE LESS ABLE TO DRAW THEIR EYEBROWS TOGETHER AND LOOK SO UNHAPPY.

THE DATA SUGGESTED THAT WHEN A PATIENT'S FACIAL EXPRESSION IS LESS SAD, THEY HAVE FEWER NEGATIVE FEELINGS. THEY MAY EVEN FEEL BETTER, BUT AS SCIENTISTS FREQUENTLY LIKE TO SAY: FURTHER STUDIES ARE NEEDED!

SOME MEN HAVE "PARALLEL PREGNANCIES".
THAT IS, THEY FEEL THE SAME SYMPTOMS OF PREGNANCY
AS THEIR PARTNERS.

YOU SHOULD PROBABLY HIBERNATE.

IN FACT, HIBERNATION COULD CHANGE THE WAY WE TREAT INFLAMMATORY DISEASES, INSOMNIA, OR TRAUMA. IT'S ALSO ABOUT THE ONLY WAY YOU'LL EVER TRAVEL IN DEEP SPACE.

BEING TICKLISH IS PRIMAL.
IT SEEMS TO HAVE EVOLVED AS A MEANS TO PROTECT US AGAINST
PARASITIC INFECTIONS.

MEN COULD BREASTFEED.
IN THEORY.

BOTH MEN AND WOMEN HAVE MAMMARY GLANDS. AND THEY
BOTH PRODUCE THE HORMONE PROLACTIN, WHICH IS NECESSARY FOR
BREASTFEEDING. BUT MEN PRODUCE LESS OF IT.

HUMANS ARE THE ONLY LIVING BEINGS WITH A CHIN.

BLUSHING IS GOOD.

WHEN WE GET RED IN THE FACE, WE'RE TELLING OTHERS THAT WE KNOW WE'VE MADE SOME SOCIAL FAUX PAS. IT'S A WAY OF PROTECTING US FROM FEELING EXCLUDED.

IN EXTREME SITUATIONS OF HUNGER, THE BRAIN
WILL START TO EAT ITSELF.

NATURAL TALENT IS A MYTH.

TALENT IS DEVELOPED THROUGH PHYSICAL AND MENTAL TRAINING,
CONSTANT MOTIVATION, AND THE PRODUCTION OF MYELIN.
MYELIN IS A SUBSTANCE IN THE CENTRAL NERVOUS SYSTEM. IT
IS PRODUCED WHEN YOU REPEAT (OR PRACTICE) PROCESSES. THAT
HELPS THE BRAIN GET "TALENTED".

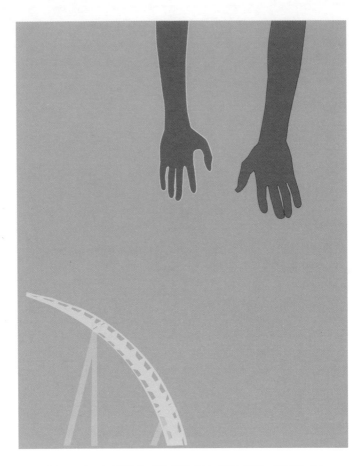

RIDING ON A ROLLER COASTER CAN HELP YOU GET RID OF KIDNEY STONES.

THE HUMAN SKELETON
RENEWS ITSELF COMPLETELY EVERY
10 YEARS.

WE DO NOT FEEL THE WEIGHT OF OUR BRAINS.

HUMAN SKIN IS A HEALTH
INDICATOR. IF YOURS STARTS
TO SMELL DIFFERENT,
GO SEE A DOCTOR.

SWEARING MAKES PAIN EASIER TO BEAR.

MOTHERS TEND TO CARRY THEIR CHILDREN ON THE LEFT.

THE RIGHT SIDE OF THE MAMMALIAN BRAIN IS RESPONSIBLE FOR
PROCESSING SOCIAL SIGNALS AND BUILDING RELATIONSHIPS.
IT IS ALSO THE SIDE OF THE BRAIN THAT RECEIVES SIGNALS FROM
THE LEFT EYE.

THAT EXPLAINS WHY BOTH HUMAN MOTHERS AND THEIR PRIMATE
COUSINS CARRY THEIR BABIES ON THE LEFT. IT ALLOWS THEM
TO KEEP A WATCHFUL AND MOTHERLY EYE ON THEIR BABY'S FACIAL
EXPRESSIONS AND, THEREFORE, THEIR NEEDS.

WATCHING HORROR FILMS BURNS CALORIES —
ABOUT A CHOCOLATE BAR'S WORTH PER MOVIE.

YOU'RE MORE LIKE YOUR DAD THAN YOU THINK.

HUMAN GENES TEND TO FAVOUR THOSE OF THE FATHER,
ESPECIALLY OVER MULTIPLE GENERATIONS.

YOU'RE ALWAYS LOOKING AT YOUR NOSE.
BUT YOUR BRAIN HIDES IT FROM VIEW.

THE MOST WIDESPREAD DISEASE IN
THE WORLD IS TOOTH DECAY.

WE'RE BORN WANTING TO DANCE.
EARLY CIVILISATIONS USED DANCE, AND OTHER COMMUNAL
MOVEMENTS, TO MAKE THEIR GROUP APPEAR LARGER
AND STRONGER. IT'S THOUGHT TO HAVE GIVEN THEM A BETTER
CHANCE OF SURVIVAL.

MULTITASKING IS IMPOSSIBLE!

WOMEN CAN HAVE ORGASMS WHILE BREASTFEEDING.

EACH AND EVERY ONE OF US
INGESTS AN AVERAGE OF 5 GRAMS
OF MICRO—PLASTICS PER WEEK.
THAT'S ABOUT THE SAME AMOUNT
OF PLASTIC THAT GOES INTO
MAKING A CREDIT CARD.

WHEN MUSICIANS PLAY TOGETHER, THEIR BRAIN WAVES SYNCHRONISE.

IT'S POSSIBLE TO USE A PERSON'S HANDWRITING TO DETECT HEALTH ISSUES.

FOR EXAMPLE, YOUR HANDWRITING CHANGES WHEN YOU'RE STRESSED. ANALYSING HANDWRITING CAN EVEN HELP DIAGNOSE MENTAL ILLNESSES AT AN EARLY STAGE.

NO MATTER WHERE WE ARE IN THE WORLD, PEOPLE EXPRESS THEIR BASIC EMOTIONS USING UNIVERSAL GESTURES.

MEN AGE MORE SLOWLY
THAN WOMEN.

YOU CANNOT KILL YOURSELF BY HOLDING YOUR BREATH.

UNDOING AGEING.

SCIENTISTS RESEARCHING HUMAN AGEING PREDICT IT WILL BE
POSSIBLE TO STOP THE BIOLOGICAL PROCESS WITHIN 30 YEARS.
WE WOULD HAVE TO STOP THE DEGENERATION OF HUMAN CELLS.
BUT, IN THEORY, A PERSON BORN TODAY COULD BECOME A LOT
OLDER THAN WE CAN IMAGINE.

WHEN YOU LISTEN TO MUSIC, YOUR HEART BEATS IN TIME
TO THE SONG.

THERE'S A BLIND SPOT IN THE HUMAN EYE WHERE THE ORGAN CANNOT RECEIVE LIGHT. BUT YOU'RE UNLIKELY TO EVER NOTICE THAT BECAUSE YOUR BRAIN COMPENSATES FOR THE LACK OF STIMULI.

EVOLUTION BIOLOGY SHOWS THAT THE HUMAN BRAIN
IS CONDITIONED TO SAVE ENERGY.

BREAST MILK IS DIFFERENT FOR BOYS AND GIRLS.

MOTHERS NATURALLY PRODUCE BREAST MILK THAT IS SPECIFIC
TO THE BIOLOGICAL SEX, AND GROWING NEEDS, OF A BABY.
BREAST MILK FOR BOYS IS HIGH IN FAT AND PROTEIN, OR ENERGY,
BREAST MILK FOR GIRLS TENDS TO BE HIGHER IN CALCIUM.

YOUR SENSE OF SMELL RESTS WHEN YOU SLEEP.

IF TWO SETS OF IDENTICAL
TWINS MIX AND HAVE BABIES,
THEIR CHILDREN WILL BE
GENETIC SIBLINGS.

STILL WONDERING WHY YOU SPLIT UP?
PERHAPS YOU WERE ALLERGIC TO YOUR EX-PARTNER. PEOPLE
CAN BE ALLERGIC TO OTHER PEOPLE, AS WELL AS TO THEMSELVES.
IT IS POSSIBLE TO BE ALLERGIC TO ONE'S OWN — OR ANOTHER
PERSON'S — HORMONES AND SPERM.

MITES LIVE IN YOUR
EYELASHES AND EYEBROWS.

MENTAL
FACTS.

YOUR FEET ARE THE MOST HONEST BIT ABOUT YOU.

IF YOU'RE TALKING TO SOMEONE AND YOU POINT YOUR FEET
IN THEIR DIRECTION, YOU SIGNAL INTEREST. BUT IF YOU POINT
YOUR FEET AWAY, IT SIGNALS A LACK OF OPPOSITE. IT MAY
INDICATE DISAGREEMENT. SO, EVEN IF YOU'RE FACING THE PERSON
YOU'RE TALKING TO, YOUR FEET ARE TELLING THEM YOU'RE
HEADING FOR THE DOOR.

NO PERSON BORN BLIND HAS EVER DEVELOPED SCHIZOPHRENIA.

HALLUCINATORY VOICES SOUND DIFFERENT FROM COUNTRY TO COUNTRY.

RESEARCH SUGGESTS THAT IF YOU HEAR SOUNDS IN YOUR HEAD,
THEY WILL DEPEND ON YOUR CULTURE AND ENVIRONMENT.
FOR INSTANCE, HALLUCINATORY VOICES IN THE USA TEND TO BE
HARSH AND THREATENING, WHILE IN AFRICAN COUNTRIES AND
INDIA THEY CAN BE FRIENDLY AND PLAYFUL.

SELFIES ON TINDER ARE TELLING.
MEN OFTEN TAKE SELFIES FROM BELOW, WHILE WOMEN
TAKE THEM FROM ABOVE. THAT MAY BE BECAUSE A PERSPECTIVE
FROM BELOW MAKES YOU LOOK TALL AND DOMINANT. AND A
PERSPECTIVE FROM ABOVE MAKES YOU LOOK SLIM. BUT THE
LATTER ALSO CONVEYS A WEAK SELF-IMAGE.

PEOPLE FIND IT EASIER TO
RECOGNISE AND INTERPRET FACIAL
EXPRESSIONS WHEN THEY
ARE IN THEIR OWN CULTURAL
ENVIRONMENTS THAN ELSEWHERE.

PEOPLE ARE OFTEN UNAWARE OF THEIR DAILY ROUTINES. WE TEND
TO DO REGULAR TASKS AUTOMATICALLY AND UNCONSCIOUSLY. THE
PHENOMENON IS CALLED HIGHWAY HYPNOSIS.

YOUR MEMORY IS DISTORTED — SAME AS EVERYONE ELSE'S.

MEMORIES LIVE ON IN OUR MINDS. THEY EVOLVE IN OUR MINDS TO THE EXTENT THAT THEY SELDOM REPRESENT WHAT REALLY HAPPENED. OUR REALITY IS A MIX OF FACT AND FANTASY. IT'S ALMOST IMPOSSIBLE TO KEEP THE TWO APART.

SOME MEN CAN HAVE AN ORGASM,
WITHOUT BEING TOUCHED.

ALZHEIMER'S PATIENTS RETAIN
A SENSE OF AESTHETICS EVEN AS
THE DISEASE PROGRESSES. A
PERSONAL SENSE OF BEAUTY
REMAINS.

MANY CHILDREN MAKE IMAGINARY FRIENDS. AND STUDIES SHOW THAT THOSE WHO DO ARE OFTEN MORE CREATIVE AND INVENTIVE THAN THOSE WHO DO NOT.

CHILDREN WHO HAVE IMAGINARY FRIENDS ALSO TEND TO DESCRIBE THEIR REAL FRIENDS BASED ON CHARACTER, RATHER THAN HOW THEY LOOK. THAT'S NOT THE NORM AMONG OTHER KIDS.

DARK HUMOUR IS A SIGN OF AN
INTELLIGENT MIND.

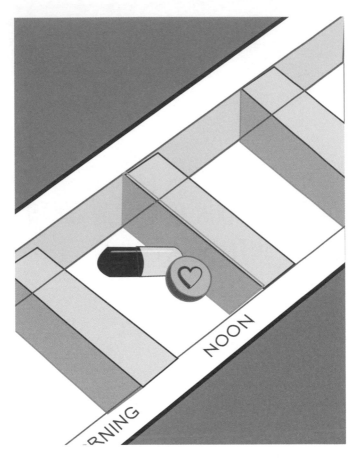

MEDICAL STUDIES SUGGEST THAT PEOPLE WITH DEPRESSION CAN
BE TREATED WITH PSYCHEDELIC DRUGS.

YOUR BRAIN IS CAPABLE OF
MAKING DECISIONS BEFORE YOU'RE
EVEN AWARE THAT YOU'VE MADE
A DECISION.

IF YOU BECOME MENTALLY ILL,
CHANCES ARE YOU WON'T REALISE IT'S HAPPENING.

BABIES CAN SENSE THE NATURE OF RELATIONSHIPS BASED ON HOW PEOPLE MAKE EACH OTHER LAUGH.

BY THE AGE OF FIVE MONTHS BABIES CAN PICK UP ON SPECIFIC SIGNALS IN LAUGHTER. THEY ARE AMAZINGLY SENSITIVE TO ACOUSTIC CUES

OUR BRAINS ARE BETTER AT FINDING CAKE THAN TOMATOES.
HUMAN SPATIAL RECALL HAS EVOLVED TO PRIORITISE HIGH—CALORIE,
ENERGY—RICH FOOD.

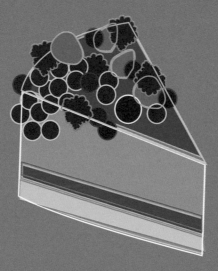

PEOPLE WHO LOSE THEIR SENSE OF SIGHT CAN REPURPOSE THE BRAIN'S VISUAL REGIONS AND USE THEM FOR LANGUAGE INSTEAD.

THE MORE ATTENTION YOU PAY TO A SITUATION,
THE FASTER YOU PERCEIVE THE PASSING OF TIME.

work

friends

dating

sports

TO FORGET IS TO PROTECT.

FORGETTING THINGS IS OFTEN CONSIDERED A MISTAKE. BUT IT'S
A VALUABLE PROCESS. AS WE ABSORB NEW INFORMATION IN A
CONTINUOUS FLOW, IT IS IMPORTANT FOR THE BRAIN TO FORGET
THINGS. IT ALLOWS THE BRAIN — AND US — TO ADAPT TO
CHANGING SITUATIONS. IT ALSO PROTECTS THE BRAIN FROM
INFORMATION OVERLOAD.

PRONOIA IS THE OPPOSITE OF PARANOIA. PEOPLE WITH PRONOIA
BELIEVE PEOPLE ARE CONSPIRING TO DO THEM GOOD.

PUNISHED BY YOUR SENSE
OF TIME.

IT'S BEEN SUGGESTED THAT PSYCHOACTIVE DRUGS COULD BE USED
TO ALTER A PRISON INMATE'S PERCEPTION OF TIME. AN ETHICIST
IN THE UK ONCE SUGGESTED THE IDEA AS AN ARTIFICIAL MEANS OF
EXTENDING OR REDUCING THE AMOUNT OF TIME A PRISONER
FEELS THEY HAVE BEEN INCARCERATED.

CHILDREN BORN WITHOUT SIGHT COVER THEIR EYES
WHEN THEY HEAR BAD NEWS.

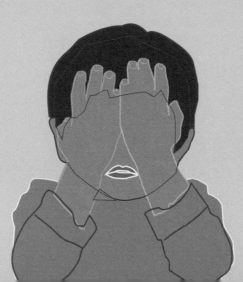

EMOTIONAL PAIN CAN HURT AS MUCH AS PHYSICAL PAIN.

IN FACT, THE BRAIN REGISTERS EMOTIONAL PAIN IN THE SAME WAY AS PHYSICAL PAIN. BOTH TYPES OF PAIN ACTIVATE THE SAME RECEPTORS IN THE BRAIN, TRIGGERING THE SAME CHEMICALS. SO, EMOTIONAL PAIN CAN FEEL JUST AS BAD AS PHYSICAL PAIN.

FEARS AND TRAUMAS CAN BE INHERITED OVER GENERATIONS.

MOST PEOPLE OVERESTIMATE THEMSELVES AND THEIR ABILITIES.

IN FACT, EVOLUTIONARY THEORY ENCOURAGES SUCH BEHAVIOUR.
PEOPLE WHO THINK HIGHLY OF THEMSELVES TEND TO TAKE
BETTER CARE OF THEMSELVES. AS A RESULT, THEIR CHANCES OF
SURVIVAL AND REPRODUCTION INCREASE AS WELL.

THE MAJORITY OF PEOPLE WHO GREW UP WITH BLACK AND WHITE
TELEVISION ALSO DREAMED IN BLACK AND WHITE.

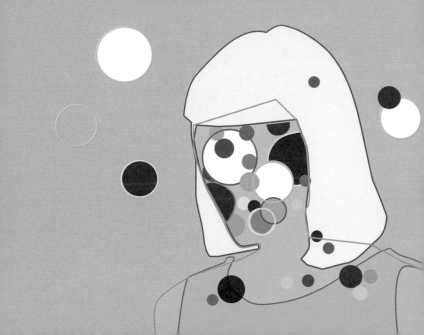

DÉJÀ—VU DÉJÀ—VU

ONE OF THE MANY EXPLANATIONS FOR FEELING LIKE YOU'RE
RELIVING A SITUATION, OR HAVING A DÉJÀ—VU, AS IT'S CALLED,
IS THAT THERE'S A DELAY BETWEEN CERTAIN BRAIN PROCESSES.

ONE PART OF YOUR BRAIN MAY HAVE FINISHED PROCESSING
NEW INFORMATION AND STORED IT IN MEMORY, BUT ANOTHER
MAY HAVE ONLY JUST REGISTERED THAT THERE'S NEW INFORMATION
TO HANDLE. WHEN THAT HAPPENS, THE BRAIN MAY FAIL TO
CATEGORISE INFORMATION PROPERLY

MEMORIES ARE BETTER THAN THE REAL THING.

THE ANATOMY OF EMOTION.

A STUDY BY EMOTION RESEARCHERS HAS SUGGESTED
THAT OUR BODIES FEEL EMOTIONS IN WAYS THAT ARE UNIVERSAL
WITHIN A CULTURE. THEY OBSERVED, FOR INSTANCE, THAT
SOME CULTURES FEEL LOVE, HAPPINESS AND PRIDE MOST
STRONGLY — AND MOST COMMONLY — IN THE UPPER BODY.

MEN ARE MORE LIKELY TO DREAM OF OTHER MEN THAN WOMEN. WOMEN DREAM EQUALLY OF BOTH SEXES. MEN TEND TO DREAM OF AGGRESSIVE ENCOUNTERS (USUALLY WITH STRANGERS), WHILE WOMEN TEND TO DREAM OF MEETING PEOPLE THEY KNOW, IN FAMILIAR ENVIRONMENTS.

YOUR BRAIN FEELS THE SORROW
OF LOVE LIKE A HEROIN ADDICT
FEELS SYMPTOMS OF WITHDRAWAL.

MULTILINGUAL PEOPLE HAVE BEEN SHOWN TO HAVE
DIFFERENT PERSONALITY PROFILES.

YOUR MEMORIES ARE EASILY MANIPULATED.

MEMORIES CAN BE MANIPULATED, ESPECIALLY WHEN THEY ARE LINKED TO REAL EXPERIENCES. A STUDY BY PSYCHOLOGISTS HAS SUGGESTED THAT CAN EVEN BE DONE WITH MEMORIES RELATING TO CRIMINAL ACTS.

YOUR FIRST NAME CAN INFLUENCE THE WAY OTHER PEOPLE PERCEIVE YOUR AGE AND PERSONALITY, AND HOW GOOD THEY THINK YOU ARE AT YOUR JOB.

A BRAIN SCAN CAN REVEAL YOUR FRIENDS.

IF YOU COMPARED THE BRAIN ACTIVITY OF TWO FRIENDS, THEY WOULD APPEAR MORE SIMILAR THAN THE BRAIN ACTIVITY OF TWO STRANGERS. THAT'S TRUE FOR BRAIN REGIONS THAT CONTROL CONCENTRATION, EMOTION AND LANGUAGE. THE SIMILARITIES IN BRAIN ACTIVITY BETWEEN FRIENDS ARE SO STRONG THAT YOU COULD TELL WHETHER TWO PEOPLE WERE FRIENDS OR NOT.

THE PANDORA EFFECT: A WARNING.
CURIOSITY WILL LEAD YOU ASTRAY FROM COMMON SENSE.

OUR FEAR AND DISGUST OF INSECTS IS INNATE.

WE HATE THE FACT THAT INSECTS CAN PENETRATE, BITE AND STING US. THEY CHALLENGE OUR SENSES OF WILL AND CONTROL.

YOU'RE MORE PRODUCTIVE WHEN YOU'RE IN A BAD MOOD.
YOU'RE LESS LIKELY TO MAKE MISTAKES, MORE FOCUSED, AND YOUR
SENSE OF JUDGEMENT IS MORE CRITICAL THAN WHEN
YOU'RE IN A GOOD MOOD.

THE FIRST NIGHT SLEEPING AWAY
FROM HOME, HALF OF YOUR BRAIN
STAYS AWAKE.

IT'S EASIER TO FALL IN LOVE ON HOLIDAY!

FEELINGS OF LOVE ON HOLIDAY MAY BE EXPLAINED AS A
MIND—BODY MIX—UP. SAY YOU EXPERIENCE SOMETHING EXCITING,
MAKING YOU FEEL PHYSICALLY UPLIFTED, WHILE AT THE SAME TIME
YOU FEEL PHYSICALLY CLOSE TO SOMEONE YOU FIND ATTRACTIVE.
IN A SITUATION LIKE THAT YOU MAY MISINTERPRET THAT
SENSE OF EXCITEMENT IN YOUR MIND WITH WHAT'S HAPPENING
IN YOUR BODY, AND THINK IT'S LOVE.

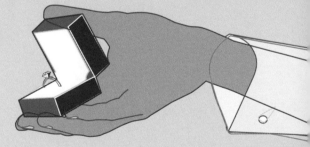

WALKING BACKWARDS CAN BOOST
YOUR SHORT-TERM MEMORY.

PSYCHOPATHS HAVE A BELOW-AVERAGE INTELLIGENCE.

IF YOU START OUT WITH
A PLAN B, YOUR PLAN A
IS DOOMED TO FAIL.

MOTHER NATURE
FACTS.

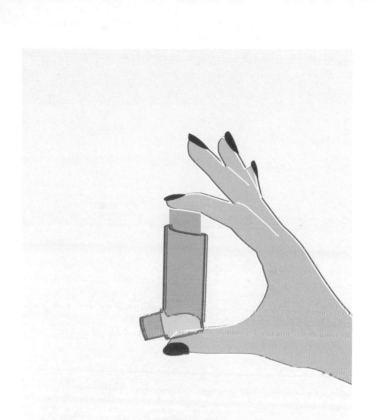

ALLERGIC TO HOUSEHOLD PETS? DID YOU KNOW THAT HUMANS
CAN CAUSE ALLERGIC REACTIONS IN DOGS AND CATS AS WELL? ONE
IN 200 DOMESTIC CATS DEVELOPS AN ALLERGY TO HUMAN HAIR
AND SKIN FLAKES. SOME EVEN GET ASTHMA.

SHY PETALS.
SOME OF US THINK PLANTS ENJOY HAVING THEIR LEAVES CARESSED.
BUT, IN FACT, IT STRESSES THEM OUT. THE HUMAN TOUCH
CAN SPARK A GENETIC DEFENCE REACTION IN PLANTS THAT HINDERS
THEIR GROWTH.

OUTER SPACE SMELLS LIKE A MIXTURE OF GUNPOWDER, FRIED STEAK, RASPBERRIES AND RUM.

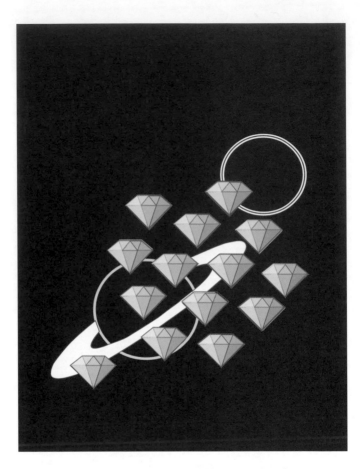

IT RAINS DIAMONDS ON SATURN AND JUPITER.

ASTRONAUTS ON THE
INTERNATIONAL SPACE STATION
GET TO WATCH 16 SUNRISES
AND 16 SUNSETS A DAY.

(IF THEY'RE NOT TOO BUSY DOING EXPERIMENTS, THAT IS.)

BATS SING LOVE SONGS, TOO, YOU KNOW.

THE HUMAN SCIENCES STUDY
MANY ANIMALS THAT AT FIRST
GLANCE HAVE LITTLE TO DO
WITH HUMANS. BUT TAKE
THE JELLYFISH TURRITOPSIS
NUTRICULA. IT IS BASICALLY
IMMORTAL BECAUSE IT CAN
REVERSE ITS BIOLOGICAL
AGEING PROCESS. AND AIN'T
THAT A HUMAN DESIRE?

WHILE YOU LOOK THAT GIFT HORSE IN THE MOUTH, IT'S LOOKING YOU IN THE EYES. HORSES CAN READ HUMAN FACIAL EXPRESSIONS AND TELL THE DIFFERENCE BETWEEN POSITIVE AND NEGATIVE EMOTIONS.

THE WAY YOU PERCEIVE BEAUTY DEPENDS ON THE SYMMETRY OF THINGS.

THE MORE SYMMETRICAL, THE MORE BEAUTIFUL.
IN EVOLUTIONARY BIOLOGY, A SENSE OF BEAUTY IS SAID TO BE
CONDITIONED BY SYMMETRY — AND WHETHER YOU THINK
THAT SOMETHING IS EDIBLE AND SAFE. SYMMETRY IS CONSIDERED AN
EVOLUTIONARY INDICATOR OF GOOD HEALTH AND STRONG GENES.

ANTHROPOLOGISTS HAVE SHOWN THAT CHIMPANZEES LIKE TO IMITATE
PEOPLE AT ZOOS AS MUCH AS PEOPLE LIKE IMITATING CHIMPANZEES.

BEAMING DOES NOT VIOLATE
ANY PHYSICAL LAW.

CATS BRING US "PRESENTS" BECAUSE THEY THINK WE ARE UNABLE
TO HUNT FOR OURSELVES.

THERE'S A PINK SNOW HIGH UP
IN SOME ALPINE REGIONS THAT
SMELLS LIKE WATERMELON.

RAINBOWS AT NIGHT ARE CALLED MOONBOWS.

THERE ARE NO COLOURS.

OUR MINDS CONJURE UP THE COLOURFUL WORLD AROUND US.
THE THINGS WE SEE HAVE NO COLOUR THEMSELVES. PLANTS ARE NOT
GREEN, BLOOD IS NOT RED AND THE OCEAN IS NOT BLUE.

COLOUR PERCEPTION DEPENDS ON WHAT SCIENTISTS CALL THE
"SCATTERING AND ABSORPTION" OF LIGHT RAYS IN THE ATMOSPHERE
AND HOW THOSE RAYS REFLECT OFF OBJECTS. THE REST IS DONE IN
OUR HEADS TO HELP US DISTINGUISH BETWEEN DIFFERENT THINGS.

THE EARTH ORBITS THE SUN AT A SPEED OF 30 KILOMETRES PER
SECOND. THAT'S 107,000 KILOMETRES PER HOUR.

HOMOSEXUALITY IS COMMON AMONG ALL ANIMALS, INCLUDING NON—HUMAN ANIMALS, LIKE BIRDS AND DOLPHINS.

ALTHOUGH, IT'S MORE PRECISE TO CALL IT SAME—SEX MATING. SOME, LIKE BONOBO APES, ARE BISEXUAL — THEY HAVE A HUGE SEXUAL APPETITE. OTHER ANIMALS ARE ASEXUAL. AQUATIC HYDRA, FOR INSTANCE, REPRODUCE WITHOUT A MATE AND CREATE PERFECT LITTLE CLONES OF THEMSELVES.

CULTURAL
FACTS.

ANTHROPOLOGISTS HAVE YET TO DISCOVER A CULTURE IN WHICH
CHILDREN DO NOT PLAY HIDE AND SEEK.

UP TO 80 PERCENT OF HUMAN CONVERSATIONS ARE
BASED ON GOSSIP.

YOU ARE GIFTED.

EVER WONDERED WHY WE FEEL OBLIGED TO ACCEPT GIFTS AND GIVE
GIFTS IN RETURN? WELL, ETHNOLOGY — THE STUDY OF CULTURE —
VIEWS THE EXCHANGE OF GIFTS AS A SOCIAL ANCHOR. WHEN WE
GIVE SOMEONE A GIFT, THAT GIFT CONTAINS A PIECE OF US. AND
WHEN THEY RECIPROCATE, WE GET A PIECE OF THEM BACK.

THE RATE OF SUICIDES IN THE GENERAL PUBLIC INCREASES
WHEN CELEBRITY SUICIDES GET REPORTED ON THE FRONT PAGES
OF NEWSPAPERS.

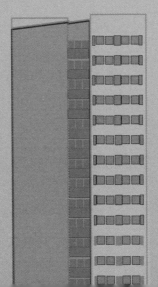

YOU ARE WORTH IT.

IF YOU COULD BUY ALL THE BASIC MATERIALS THAT
WENT INTO MAKING YOUR PHYSICAL BODY, YOU WOULD COST
BETWEEN €1,500 AND €1,600.

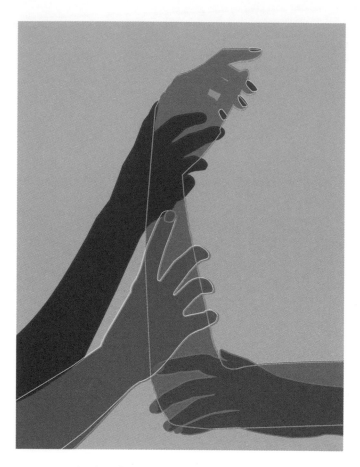

PEOPLE ARE NOT MONOGAMOUS BY NATURE.
MONOGAMY IS A CULTURAL INVENTION.

TECHNOLOGY CHANGES US.

OUR AGE OF HAND-GESTURE TECHNOLOGY IS CHANGING
US PHYSICALLY. OUR HANDS WILL BE DIFFERENT IN
FUTURE — THE SAME WAY THAT CUTLERY CHANGED OUR MOUTHS.

THERE IS A TEDDY BEAR FOR TRAUMATISED CHILDREN ON THE BACK SEAT OF EVERY POLICE CAR IN THE NETHERLANDS.

SUNGLASSES WERE ORIGINALLY DESIGNED FOR CHINESE JUDGES TO HIDE THEIR FACIAL EXPRESSIONS IN COURT.

SIGN LANGUAGE HAS DIALECTS AND REGIONAL EXPRESSIONS.

THE MOST COMMON CAUSE OF DEATH AMONG CHILDREN IN JAPAN IS SUICIDE.

OFTEN, IT'S DOWN TO PROBLEMS AT SCHOOL — TOO MUCH PRESSURE TO DO WELL, OR BULLYING. UNLIKE IN OTHER COUNTRIES, SUICIDE IS NOT GENERALLY CONSIDERED BAD IN JAPAN. INSTEAD, IT'S SEEN AS A WAY OF TAKING RESPONSIBILITY FOR YOUR ACTIONS, OR SEEKING FORGIVENESS. SUICIDE IS DEEPLY ROOTED IN JAPANESE CULTURE.

IN HONG KONG, IT IS LEGAL FOR WOMEN TO KILL THEIR HUSBANDS
IF THEIR MEN ARE FOUND TO HAVE COMMITTED ADULTERY.
BUT THEY ARE ONLY ALLOWED TO USE THEIR HANDS TO DO THE
MURDEROUS DEED.

PEOPLE WHO FIND PARTNERS
ONLINE GET MARRIED FASTER
THAN COUPLES WHO MEET IN
"REAL LIFE".

AGE—OTORI.
A JAPANESE EXPRESSION FOR WHEN YOU LOOK WORSE AFTER A VISIT
TO THE HAIRDRESSER THAN YOU DID BEFORE.

ANIMAL NOISES GET VOCALISED DIFFERENTLY IN DIFFERENT CULTURES.

FOR EXAMPLE, ENGLISH DOGS GO "WOOF!"
WHILE SPANISH DOGS GO "GUAU GUAU!"
NEXT DOOR IN PORTUGAL, THEY GO "OW OW!"
IN FRANCE, IT'S "OUAF OUAF!"
BUT IN ITALY "BAU BAU!"
SOUTH KOREAN DOGS ARE ALL ABOUT THE "MUNG MUNG!"
WHILE IN RUSSIA THEY GROWL "GAV GAV!"
IN TURKEY, IT'S "HEV HEV!"
DUTCH DOGS BARK "BLAH BLAF!",
WHILE IT'S A "WAN WAN!" SITUATION IN JAPAN.
AND ICELANDIC DOGS?
THEY DO AN EERILY ENGLISH "VOFF VOFF!".

DID YOU KNOW THAT THE WORLD FAMOUS "MADE IN GERMANY" TAG WAS ORIGINALLY INTENDED AS A WARNING AGAINST GERMAN PRODUCTS? THE BRITISH INTRODUCED IT TO WARN SHOPPERS AGAINST INFERIOR OR COPIED PRODUCTS THAT WERE MADE IN GERMANY.

PARIS SYNDROME.

MANY ASIANS DREAM OF A ONCE-IN-A-LIFETIME TRIP TO PARIS.
BUT WHEN THEY GET THERE, THE REALITY OF THE PLACE
SELDOM LIVES UP TO THEIR EXPECTATIONS. SOME VISITORS
EXPERIENCE A SENSE OF SHOCK SO DEEP THAT IT HAS BEEN SAID
TO LEAD TO DEPRESSION AND ANXIETY DISORDERS.

WE SHAKE HANDS TO SHOW THAT WE ARE UNARMED.

THINK BLUE IS THE "NATURAL" COLOUR FOR BOYS AND THAT PINK IS FOR GIRLS?

WELL, GENDER STEREOTYPES SWITCH WITH THE TIMES. IN THE EARLY 1900s, LOTS OF BOYS WORE PINK AS IT WAS CONSIDERED A STRONG COLOUR, WHILE GIRLS WORE A "DELICATE AND DAINTY" BLUE.

THE MORE PEOPLE THAT WITNESS AN EMERGENCY SITUATION,
THE LESS LIKELY IT IS THAT ANY OF THEM WILL HELP.

THE SOUND YOUR SNEEZE
MAKES DEPENDS ON THE LANGUAGE
YOU SPEAK.

IN THE MIDDLE AGES, PEOPLE YAWNED WITH THEIR HANDS IN FRONT
OF THEIR MOUTHS BECAUSE THEY BELIEVED THAT OPEN MOUTHS LET
THEIR SOULS ESCAPE AND LET DEMONS GET IN.

IT'S COMMONLY THOUGHT THAT SUICIDE RATES ARE HIGHEST DURING THE DARKER MONTHS.

BUT RESEARCH SUGGESTS THAT PEOPLE ARE MORE LIKELY TO KILL THEMSELVES IN SPRING AND EARLY SUMMER. SOME PSYCHOLOGISTS SAY ALLERGIC REACTIONS CAN WORSEN FEELINGS OF DEPRESSION. OTHERS SAY IT'S THE POSITIVE MOOD OF THOSE BRIGHTER MONTHS THAT CAN INTENSIFY A DEPRESSED PERSON'S SENSE OF SADNESS.

HELLO UNIVERSE!

VOYAGER I AND 2 ARE SPACECRAFT THAT NASA LAUNCHED IN 1977. THE IDEA WAS TO FLY DEEP INTO THE UNIVERSE, BEYOND OUR SOLAR SYSTEM, WITH GREETINGS FROM EARTH FOR EXTRATERRESTRIAL LIFEFORMS. WE WANTED TO TELL THEM ABOUT OUR HUMAN CIVILISATIONS. THE SPACECRAFT CARRY A GOLDEN RECORD CALLED THE SOUNDS OF EARTH. IT HOLDS GREETINGS IN 55 LANGUAGES, 27 PIECES OF MUSIC — FROM BACH TO THE BEATLES — AND RECORDINGS OF HUMAN LAUGHTER, DOGS BARKING AND THE GENTLE SOUND OF A KISS.

EARTH IS MORE PEACEFUL TODAY THAN AT ANY OTHER TIME
IN HUMAN HISTORY.

p 7   Bever, L. (2016). How these twins turned out to have different fathers. The Washington Post.
        https://perma.cc/P3BW-WAGB (Page last reviewed: May 2021).

p 8   Gotlib, T., Samoliński, B., & Arcimowicz, M. (2002). Spontaneous changes of nasal patency,
        the nasal cycle, classification, frequency, and clinical significance. Otolaryngol Pol.
        https://perma.cc/XL6D-ML42 (Page last reviewed: May 2021).

p 9   Havas, D. A., Glenberg, A. M., Gutowski, K. A., Lucarelli, M. J., & R. J. Davidson. Cosmetic
        Use of Botulinum Toxin-A Affects Processing of Emotional Language. Psychological Science.
        https://doi.org/10.1177/0956797610374742

p 10   Volponi, A. A., Zaugg, L. K., Neves, V., Liu, Y., & Sharpe, P. T. (2018). Tooth Repair and
        Regeneration. Current Oral Health Reports. https://doi.org/10.1007/s40496-018-0196-9

p 11   Macaulay, D. (2015). Eye: How It Works. Square Fish.

p 12   Stromberg, J. (2013). The Microscopic Structures of Dried Human Tears. Smithsonian
        Magazine. https://perma.cc/KZJ7-2RZC (Page last reviewed: May 2021).

p 13   Abbott, D. (2016). What brain regions control our language? And how do we know this?
        The Conversation. https://perma.cc/ZVS3-8RDU (Page last reviewed: May 2021).
        Steinberg, D. (2020). Understanding What Makes A Swear Effective Could Lead To
        Advances In Treating Brain Injury. Temple University College of Public Health.
        https://perma.cc/YNT4-42XP (Page last reviewed: May 2021).

p 14   Zittlau, J. (2019). Wie schlafen Tiere? Rücken kann nicht entzücken. taz.
        https://perma.cc/G3UT-VUAL (Page last reviewed: May 2021).

p 15   Haas, M. (2010). Mir entgeht kein Gesichtsausdruck. Süddeutsche Zeitung.
        https://perma.cc/58CJ-M4RW (Page last reviewed: May 2021).
        Matlock, G. (2006). Handbuch der Körperpsychotherapie. Stuttgart, New York.

p 16   Love, T., Laier, C., Brand, M., Hatch, L., & Hajela, R. (2015). Neuroscience of Internet
        Pornography Addiction: A Review and Update. Behav Sci. https://doi.org/10.3390/bs5030388
        Kelland, K. (2014). In the brain, sex addiction looks the same as drug addiction. Reuters.
        https://perma.cc/P259-CBRM (Page last reviewed: May 2021).

p 17   MacCormack, J. K., & Lindquist, K. A. (2019). Feeling hangry?
        When hunger is conceptualized as emotion. American Psychology Association PsycArticles.
        https://doi.org/10.1037/emo0000422

p 18   Kramer, M. (2013). Strange But True: Astronauts Get Taller in Space. Space.com.
        https://perma.cc/DBN6-47VN (Page last reviewed: May 2021).

p 19   Makunts, T., Wollmer, M. A., & Abagyan, R. (2020). Postmarketing safety surveillance
        data reveals antidepressant effects of botulinum toxin across various indications and
        injection sites. Scientific Reports. https://doi.org/10.1038/s41598-020-69773-7

p 20   Brennan, A., Ayers, S., Ahmed, H., & Marshall-Lucette, S. (2007). A critical review of the
        Couvade syndrome: the pregnant male. Journal of Reproductive and Infant Psychology.
        https://doi.org/10.1080/02646030701467207

p 21   Hamblin, J. (2020). You Could Probably Hibernate. The Atlantic.
        https://perma.cc/HH92-GF4C (Page last reviewed: May 2021).

p 22   Schindler, S.-S. (2008). Lachen und leiden. stern.
        https://perma.cc/YW5C-W4E5 (Page last reviewed: May 2021).

p 23   Swaminathan, N. (2007). Strange but True: Males Can Lactate. Scientific American.
        https://perma.cc/ZD5V-TCMG (Page last reviewed: May 2021).
        NHS Foundation Trust (2019). Breastfeeding: the first few days. https://tinyurl.com/pkmnbf
        (Page last reviewed: May 2021).

p 24   Pampush, J. D., & Daegling, D. J. (2016). The enduring puzzle of the human chin.
        Evolutionary Anthropology. https://doi.org/10.1002/evan.21471

p 25   Edelmann, R. J. (2001). Blushing. In Crozier, W. R., & Alden, L. E. (Eds.).
        International handbook of social anxiety: Concepts, research and interventions relating
        to the self and shyness. John Wiley & Sons Ltd.

p 26   Kaushik, S., Rodriguez-Navarro, J. A., Arias, E., Kiffin, R., Sahu, S., Schwartz, G. J.,
        Cuervo, A. M., & Singh, R. (2011). Autophagy in Hypothalamic AgRP Neurons Regulates
        Food Intake and Energy Balance. Cell Metabolism.
        https://doi.org/10.1016/j.cmet.2011.06.008

p 27   Coyle, D. (2009). Die Talent-Lüge: Warum wir (fast) alles erreichen können. Bastei Lübbe.

p 28   Mitchell, M. A., & Wartinger, D. D. (2016). Validation of a Functional Pyelocalyceal Renal
        Model for the Evaluation of Renal Calculi Passage While Riding a Roller Coaster. The
        Journal of the American Osteopathic Association. https://doi.org/10.7556/jaoa.2016.128

p 29   Kunsch, K. (2006). Der Mensch in Zahlen. Spektrum Akademischer Verlag.

p 30   Namdev, V. (2017). The Reason why we don't feel the weight of Brain. Medium.
        https://perma.cc/JU6H-Y6EM (Page last reviewed: May 2021).

p 31   Olsson, M. J., Lundström, J. N., Kimball, B. A., Gordon, A. R., Karshikoff, B., Hosseini, N.,
        Sorjonen, K., Olgard Höglund, C., Solares, C., Soop, A., Axelsson, J., & Lekander, M.
        (2014). The Scent of Disease: Human Body Odor Contains an Early Chemosensory Cue
        of Sickness. Psychological Science. https://doi.org/10.1177/0956797613515681

p 32   Stephens, R., Atkins, J., & Kingston, A. (2005). Swearing as a response to pain.
        Neuroreport. https://pubmed.ncbi.nlm.nih.gov/19590391/

p 33   Karenina, K., Giljov, A., Ingram, J., Rowntree, V. J., Malashichev, Y. (2017).
        Lateralization of mother-infant interactions in a diverse range of mammal species.
        Nature Ecology & Evolution. https://doi.org/10.1038/s41559-016-0030

p 34   Child, B. (2012). Scare yourself thin: horror movies help burn calories, study finds.
        The Guardian. https://perma.cc/8UWS-5BJ6 (Page last reviewed: May 2021).

p 35   Crowley, J. J., Zhabotynsky, V., and others (2015). Analyses of allele-specific
        gene expression in highly divergent mouse crosses identifies pervasive allelic imbalance.
        Nature Genetics. https://doi.org/10.1038/ng.3222

p 36   Payne, K. (2013). Your Hidden Censor: What Your Mind Will Not Let You See. Scientific
        American. https://perma.cc/SR7B-6X6N (Page last reviewed: May 2021).

p 37   National Institute of Dental and Craniofacial Research (2018). Dental Caries (Tooth Decay).
        https://perma.cc/W9YT-LYPP (Page last reviewed: May 2021).

p 38   Singer, T. (2017). Does Dancing Just Feel Good, or Did It Help Early Humans Survive? Scientific American. https://tinyurl.com/x9uvy678 (Page last reviewed: May 2021).

p 39   Goldhill, O. (2015). Multitasking is scientifically impossible, so give up now. The Telegraph. https://perma.cc/L52Y-HZGJ (Page last reviewed: May 2021).

p 40   Alder, E. M. (1989). 7 Sexual behaviour in pregnancy, after childbirth and during breast-feeding. Baillière's Clinical Obstetrics and Gynaecology. https://doi.org/10.1016/S0950-3552(89)80066-5

p 41   WWF (2019). Aufnahme von Mikroplastik aus der Umwelt beim Menschen. Eine Analyse für WWF von Dalberg und der University of Newcastle, Australia. https://perma.cc/GWZ2-EUBY (Page last reviewed: May 2021).

p 42   Sänger, J., Müller, V., & Lindenberger, U. (2012). Intra- and interbrain synchronization and network properties when playing guitar in duets. Frontiers in Human Neuroscience. https://doi.org/10.3389/fnhum.2012.00312

p 43   Vessio, G. (2019). Dynamic Handwriting Analysis for Neurodegenerative Disease Assessment: A Literary Review. Applied Science. https://doi.org/10.3390/app9214666

p 44   Ekman, P. (2020). Facial Action Coding System. https://perma.cc/X5MX-33Z5 (Page last reviewed: May 2021).

p 45   Graves, B. M., Strand, M., & Lindsay, A. R. (2006). A reassessment of sexual dimorphism in human senescence: Theory, evidence, and causation. American Journal of Human Biology. https://doi.org/10.1002/ajhb.20488

p 46   Parkes, M. J. (2005). Breath-holding and its breakpoint. Experimental Physiology. https://doi.org/10.1113/expphysiol.2005.031625

p 47   Honey, C. (2018). Niemals unsterblich, aber ewig jung. DIE ZEIT. https://perma.cc/JX5Y-SJFN (Page last reviewed: May 2021).

p 48   Bernardi, L., Porta, C., Casucci, G., Balsamo R., Bernardi, N. F., Fogari, R., & Sleight, P. (2009). Dynamic Interactions Between Musical, Cardiovascular, and Cerebral Rhythms in Humans. Circulation. https://doi.org/10.1161/CIRCULATIONAHA.108.806174

p 49   Hunziker, H.-W. (2006). Im Auge des Lesers: Foveale und periphere Wahrnehmung. Vom Buchstabieren zur Lesefreude. transmedia Verlag Stäubli Verlag AG.

p 50   Cheval, B., Tipura, E. Burra, N., Frossard, J., Chanal, J., Orsholits, D., Radel, R., & Boisgontier, M. P. (2018). Avoiding sedentary behaviors requires more cortical resources than avoiding physical activity: An EEG study. Neuropsychologia. https://doi.org/10.1016/j.neuropsychologia.2018.07.029

p 51   Hinde, K. (2017). What we don't know about mother's milk. TED Talk. https://perma.cc/GDE3-BEJ6 (Page last reviewed: May 2021).

p 52   Carskadon, M. A., & Herz, R. S. (2004). Minimal olfactory perception during sleep: why odor alarms will not work for humans. Sleep. https://pubmed.ncbi.nlm.nih.gov/15164891/

p 53   Onyenucheya, A. (2018). Children from identical parents are genetic siblings. The Guardian. https://perma.cc/HRD7-HNMD (Page last reviewed: May 2021).

p 54   Waldinger, M. D., Meinardi, M. M. H. M., Zwinderman, A, H , & Schweitzer, D. H. (2011). Postorgasmic Illness Syndrome (POIS) in 45 Dutch Caucasian Males: Clinical

Characteristics and Evidence for an Immunogenic Pathogenesis (Part 1). The Journal of Sexual Medicine. https://doi.org/10.1111/j.1743-6109.2010.02166.x

Ludman, B. G. (1999). Human Seminal Plasma Protein Allergy: A Diagnosis Rarely Considered. Principles & Practice. https://doi.org/10.1111/j.1552-6909.1999.tb02003.x

Goldbeck, C. (2019). Kann man gegen andere Menschen allergisch sein? Quarks.de. https://perma.cc/B8KZ-JRQM (Page last reviewed: May 2021).

p 55   Engelhaupt, E. (2020). Mini-Mitbewohner: In unseren Gesichtsporen leben Milben. National Geographic. https://perma.cc/8UJ9-PH5G (Page last reviewed: May 2021).

MENTAL FACTS

p 59   Parvez, H. (2015). Body language: Truth of the pointing foot. PsychMechanics. https://perma.cc/SJ4K-DX4Y (Page last reviewed: May 2021).

p 60   Morgan, V. A., Clark, M., Crewe, J., Valuri, G., Mackey, D. A., Badcock, J. C., & Jablensky, A. (2018). Congenital blindness is protective for schizophrenia and other psychotic illness. A whole-population study. Schizophrenia Research. https://doi.org/10.1016/j.schres.2018.06.061

p 61   Parker, C. B. (2014). Hallucinatory 'voices' shaped by local culture. Stanford News. https://perma.cc/9NWC-Z2H3 (Page last reviewed: May 2021).

p 62   Sedgewick, J. R., Flath, M. E., & Elias, L. J. (2017). Presenting Your Best Self(ie): The Influence of Gender on Vertical Orientation of Selfies on Tinder. Frontiers in Psychology. https://doi.org/10.3389/fpsyg.2017.00604

p 63   Broszinsky-Schwabe, E. (2011). Interkulturelle Kommunikation: Missverständnisse und Verständigung. VS Verlag für Sozialwissenschaften.

p 64   Underwood, G. (2005). Traffic and Transport Psychology. Elsevier Science.

p 65   McRaney, D. (2012). Ich denke, also irre ich: Wie unser Gehirn uns jeden Tag täuscht. mvg Verlag.

Ucsnay, J. (2020). Gedächtnis. Planet Wissen. https://perma.cc/P776-JYD3 (Page last reviewed: May 2021).

p 66   Weiss, S. (2017). Yes, You Can Get Off Without Being Touched – And Here's What It's Like. Bustle. https://perma.cc/CQ8E-MCSV (Page last reviewed: May 2021).

p 67   Graham, D. J., Stockinger, S., & Leder, H. (2013). An island of stability: art images and natural scenes – but not natural faces – show consistent esthetic response in Alzheimer's-related dementia. Frontiers in Psychology. https://doi.org/10.3389/fpsyg.2013.00107

p 68   Taylor, M. (1999). Imaginary Companions and the Children Who Create Them. Oxford University Press.

p 69   Willinger, U., Hergovich, A., Schmoeger, M., Deckert, M., Stoettner, S., Bunda, I., Witting, A., Seidler, M., Moser, R., Kacena, S., Jaeckle, D., Loader, B., Mueller, C., & Auff, E. (2017). Cognitive and emotional demands of black humour processing: the role of

intelligence, aggressiveness and mood. Cognitive Processing.
https://doi.org/10.1007/s10339-016-0789-y

p 70   Unknown author (2017). LSD dämpft Angstgefühle. Neue Zürcher Zeitung.
https://perma.cc/QA7Z-NXXU (Page last reviewed: May 2021).

p 71   Soon, C. S., Brass, M., Heinze, H.-J., & Haynes, J.-D. (2008). Unconscious determinants
of free decisions in the human brain. Nature Neuroscience. https://doi.org/10.1038/nn.2112

p 73   Vouloumanos, A., & Bryant, G. A. (2019). Five-month-old infants detect affiliation in
colaughter. Scientific Reports. https://doi.org/10.1038/s41598-019-38954-4

p 74   de Vries, R., Morquecho-Campos, P., de Vet, E., de Rijk, M., Postma, E., de Graaf, K.,
Engel, B., & Boesveldt, S. (2020). Human spatial memory implicitly prioritizes high-calorie
foods. Scientific Reports. https://doi.org/10.1038/s41598-020-72570-x

p 75   Van Ackeren, M. J., Barbero, F. M., Mattioni, S., Bottini, R., & Collignon, O. (2018).
Neuronal populations in the occipital cortex of the blind synchronize to the temporal
dynamics of speech. eLife. https://doi.org/10.7554/eLife.31640.001

p 76   Schwarz, M. A., Winkler, I., & Sedlmeier, P. (2013). The heart beat does not make us tick:
The impacts of heart rate and arousal on time perception. Attention, Perception,
& Psychophysics. https://doi.org/10.3758/s13414-012-0387-8

p 77   Korte, M. (2018). Warum wir vergessen. Spektrum.de. https://perma.cc/MV6N-CAUC
(Page last reviewed: May 2021).

p 78   Oxford University Press (2020). Definition of pronoia. Lexico.com.
https://perma.cc/X7SB-K5HH (Page last reviewed: May 2021).

p 79   Wearden, J. H., & Penton-Voak, I. S. (1995). Feeling the heat: body temperature and the
rate of subjective time, revisited. National Center for Biotechnology Information.
https://pubmed.ncbi.nlm.nih.gov/7597195/
Love, D. (2014). Future Mind-Altering Drugs Could Make Prisoners Think They're In Jail For
1,000 Years. Business Insider. https://perma.cc/6Z54-QEME (Page last reviewed: May 2021).

p 80   Navarro, J. (2010). Menschen lesen: Ein FBI-Agent erklärt, wie man Körpersprache
entschlüsselt. mvg Verlag.

p 81   Fogel, A. (2012). Emotional and Physical Pain Activate Similar Brain Regions.
Where does emotion hurt in the body? Psychology Today. https://perma.cc/DW94-3RZG
(Page last reviewed: May 2021).

p 82   Henriques, M. (2019). Can the legacy of trauma be passed down the generations? BBC.
https://perma.cc/9DVR-Q35Q (Page last reviewed: May 2021).

p 83   Johnson, D. D. P., & Fowler, J. H. (2011). The evolution of overconfidence. Nature.
https://doi.org/10.1038/nature10384

p 84   Murzyn, E. (2008). Do we only dream in colour? A comparison of reported dream colour
in younger and older adults with different experiences of black and white media.
Consciousness and Cognition. https://pubmed.ncbi.nlm.nih.gov/18845457/

p 85   Teale, J. C., & O'Connor, A. R. (2015). What is Déjà Vu? Scientific American.
https://perma.cc/B7XL-B5QH (Page last reviewed: May 2021).

p 86   Pohl, R. F. (2016). Cognitive Illusions. Intriguing Phenomena In Judgement, Thinking
and Memory. Routledge.

p 87   Nummenmaa, L., Glerean, E., Hari, R., & Hietanen, J. K. (2013). Bodily maps of emotions. Proceedings of the National Academy of Sciences of the United States of America. https://doi.org/10.1073/pnas.1321664111 (Page last reviewed: May 2021).

p 88   McNamara, P. (2011). The Dreams of Men and Women. Men are more physically aggressive in their dreams than are women. Psychology Today. https://perma.cc/J82X-VNKF (Page last reviewed: May 2021).

p 89   Hausen, J. (2016). Wissenschaftlich erklärt, warum Liebeskummer uns so weh tut. VICE. https://perma.cc/4JQU-4GUQ (Page last reviewed: May 2021).

p 90   Dewaele, J.-M., & Botes, E. (2019). Does multilingualism shape personality? An exploratory investigation. International Journal of Bilingualism. https://doi.org/10.1177/1367006919888581

p 91   Kaplan, R. L., Van Damme, I., Levine, L. J., & Loftus, E. F. (2015). Emotion and False Memory. Emotion Review. https://doi.org/10.1177/1754073915601228
Shaw, J., & Porter, S. (2015). Constructing Rich False Memories of Committing Crime. Psychological Science. https://doi.org/10.1177/0956797614562862

p 92   Newman, L. S., Tan, M., Caldwell, T. L., Duff, K. J., & Winer, E. S. (2018). Name Norms: A Guide to Casting Your Next Experiment. Personality and Social Psychology Bulletin. https://doi.org/10.1177/0146167218769858

p 93   Parkinson, C., Kleinbaum, A. M., & Wheatley, T. (2018). Similar neural responses predict friendship. Nature Communications. https://doi.org/10.1038/s41467-017-02722-7

p 94   Hsee, C. K., & Ruan, B. (2016). The Pandora Effect: The Power and Peril of Curiosity. Psychological Science. https://doi.org/10.1177/0956797616631733

p 95   Lockwood, J. A. (2013). The Infested Mind: Why humans Fear, Loathe, and Love insects. Oxford University Press.

p 96   Gabel, M. S., & McAuley, T. (2018). Does mood help or hinder executive functions? Reactivity may be the key. Personality and Individual Differences. https://doi.org/10.1016/j.paid.2018.02.027
Smyth, P. (2018). A bad mood may help your brain with everyday tasks. University of Waterloo News. https://perma.cc/JZ7W-SADB (Page last reviewed: May 2021).

p 97   Tamaki, M., Won Bang, J., Watanabe, T., & Sasaki, Y. (2016). Night Watch in One Brain Hemisphere during Sleep Associated with the First-Night Effect in Humans. Current Biology. https://doi.org/10.1016/j.cub.2016.02.063

p 98   Dutton, D. G., & Aron, A. P. (1974). Some evidence for heightened sexual attraction under conditions of high anxiety. Journal of Personality and Social Psychology. https://doi.org/10.1037/h0037031

p 99   Aksentijevic, A., Brandt, K. R., Tsakanikos, E., & Thorpe, M. J. A. (2019). It takes me back: The mnemonic time-travel effect. Cognition. https://doi.org/10.1016/j.cognition.2018.10.007

p 100   Sánchez de Ribera, O., Kavish, N., Katz, I. M., & Boutwell, B. B. (2019). Untangling intelligence, psychopathy, antisocial personality disorder, & conduct problems: A meta-analytic review. European Journal of Personality. https://doi.org/10.1101/100693

p 101   Milkman, K., & Shin, J. (2016). Having a "Plan B" Can Hurt Your Chances of Success. Scientific American. https://perma.cc/WX5P-UP26 (Page last reviewed: May 2021).

p 105   University of Edinburgh. (2005). Asthmatic Cats May Be Allergic To Humans, Say Vets. Science News. https://perma.cc/8ACL-R7WR (Page last reviewed: May 2021).

p 106   Xu, Y., Berkowitz, O., Narsai, R., De Clerq, I., Hooi, M., Bulone, V., Van Breusegem, F., Whelan, J., & Wang, Y. (2018). Mitochondrial function modulates touch signalling in Arabidopsis thaliana. The Plant Journal. https://doi.org/10.1111/tpj.14183

p 107   Kim, A. (2020). This is what space smells like. CNN. https://perma.cc/4SYX-UUN9 (Page last reviewed: May 2021).

p 108   Fazekas, A. (2013). Diamonds Stud the Atmospheres of Saturn and Jupiter. National Geographic. https://perma.cc/RQQ2-NJVZ (Page last reviewed: May 2021).

p 109   Ranga, D. (2012). Der Tag, an dem die Sonne sechzehn Mal aufging. Eine lange Nacht über Menschen im Weltall. Deutschlandfunk. https://perma.cc/MU8X-BB3B (Page last reviewed: May 2021).

p 110   The University of Texas at Austin College of Natural Sciences (2009). Bats Sing Love Songs. https://perma.cc/38UC-HMPS (Page last reviewed: May 2021).

p 111   Piraino, S., Boero, F., Aeschbach, B., & Schmid, V. (1996). Reversing the Life Cycle: Medusae Transforming into Polyps and Cell Transdifferentiation in Turritopsis nutricula (Cnidaria, Hydrozoa). The Biological Bulletin. https://doi.org/10.2307/1543022

p 112   Smith, A. V., Proops, L., Grounds, K., Wathan, J., & McComb, K. (2016). Functionally relevant responses to human facial expressions of emotion in the domestic horse (Equus caballus). The Royal Society Publishing. https://doi.org/10.1098/rsbl.2016.0907

p 113   Sagmeister, S., & Walsh, J. (2019). Beauty. Exhibition at Museum für Angewandte Kunst, Frankfurt/Main. https://perma.cc/37V5-79EE (Page last reviewed: May 2021). Eco, U. (2014). Die Geschichte der Schönheit. Carl Hanser Verlag.

p 114   Sauqiun, O.A., & Persson, T. (2018). Chimps like to copy human visitors to the zoo – Ig Nobel Prize. The Conversation. https://perma.cc/J4WZ-HMK6 (Page last reviewed: May 2021).

p 115   Blaschke, J. (2011). Ist Beamen möglich? Max Planck-Institut für Dynamik und Selbstorganisation. https://perma.cc/8WNY-KNL6 (Page last reviewed: May 2021).

p 116   Taylor, D. (2020). Cats bring humans "presents" because they think we can't hunt for ourselves. The Golden Star. https://perma.cc/56YB-H3L6 (Page last reviewed: May 2021).

p 117   Frazer, J. (2013). Wonderful Things: Don't Eat the Pink Snow. Scientific American. https://perma.cc/MGN3-YJPF (Page last reviewed: May 2021).

p 118   Benningfield, D. (2007). Mondbögen. Deutschlandfunk. https://perma.cc/EK5Y-HCNW (Page last reviewed: February 2021).

p 119   NASA Science (2021). Ocean Color. https://perma.cc/WE9U-KB9D (Page last reviewed: May 2021). Gegenfurtner, K. R. (2020) Farbwahrnehmung. Abteilung Allgemeine Psychologie Justus-Liebig Universität Gießen. https://perma.cc/XS8A-RM8D (Page last reviewed: May 2020).

p 120   Astronomy Department at Cornell University (2016). At what speed does the Earth move around the Sun? https://perma.cc/C78M-AM3F (Page last reviewed: May 2021).

p 121   Owen, J. (2004). Homosexual Activity Among Animals Stirs Debate. National Geographic. https://perma.cc/3MMU-N82P (Page last reviewed: May 2021).
Hogenboom, M. (2015). Are there any homosexual animals? BBC. https://perma.cc/ESN5-8RG5 (Page last reviewed: May 2021).

CULTURAL FACTS

p 125   Rastegarpour, A. (2011). A Cross-cultural Comparison of Objectivity in Childhood Games: Iran and the United States. Indian Journal of Psychological Medicine. https://doi.org/10.4103/0253-7176.92049

p 126   Kenniff, S. (2010). Stop Effing Yourself: A Survivor's Guide to Life's Biggest Screw-ups. HCI.

p 127   Godelier, M. (1999). Das Rätsel der Gabe. Verlag C.H. Beck.

p 128   Niederkrotenthaler, T. (2020). Association between suicide reporting in the media and suicide: systematic review and meta-analysis. BMJ. https://doi.org/10.1136/bmj.m575

p 129   Vollmer, J. (2014). Blut, Nieren, Haare, Leben — So viel ist dein Körper wert. VICE. https://perma.cc/6VLD-24KY (Page last reviewed: May 2021).

p 130   Vergin, J. (2018). Monogamie ist nur eine Erfindung. Deutsche Welle. https://perma.cc/Z52P-JXX3 (Page last reviewed: May 2021).

p 131   Leader, D. (2016). How technology is changing our hands. The Guardian. https://perma.cc/FN2S-CDL9 (Page last reviewed: May 2021).
Leader, D. (2017). Hands: What We Do with Them — and Why? Hamish Hamilton.

p 132   Dutch Police (2020). Uniform en uitrusting. https://perma.cc/4H3Q-JF3R (Page last reviewed: May 2021).

p 133   Taylor, D. (2020). Sunglasses were originally designed for Chinese judges to hide their facial expressions in court. Vernon Morning Star. https://perma.cc/B9JA-UGE8 (Page last reviewed: May 2021).

p 134   Sze, F., Isma, S., Suwiryo, A. I., Wijaya, L. L., Bharato, A. K., Satryawan, I. (2015). Differentiating 'dialect' and 'language' in sign languages: A case study of two signing varieties in Indonesia. Asia-Pacific Language Variation. https://doi.org/10.1075/aplv.1.2.04sze

p 135   Whitman, E. (2015). Japan School Children Suicides: After Vacation, Many Young Students Kill Themselves, Study Finds. International Business Times. https://perma.cc/4S77-2U29 (Page last reviewed: May 2021).
Wingfield-Hayes, R. (2015). Why does Japan have such a high suicide rate? BBC News. https://perma.cc/6LSJ-YHPJ (Page last reviewed: May 2021).

p 136   Odongo, D. (2013). Hong Kong law allows wife to kill a cheating hubby. The Nairobian. https://perma.cc/BF4R-AZKX (Page last reviewed: May 2021).

p 137   Ferdman, R. A. (2016). How well online dating works, according to someone who has been studying it for years. The Washington Post. https://perma.cc/M3YB-5YR8 (Page last reviewed: May 2021).

p 138   Nguyen, J. (2020). 11 Untranslatable Words from Many Different Languages. Medium. https://perma.cc/XGU2-LVWT (Page last reviewed: May 2021).

p 139   Stiftung Haus der kleinen Forscher (2019). Klänge und Geräusche. Akustische Phänomene mit Kita- und Grundschulkindern entdecken. https://perma.cc/9SG3-HEU7 (Page last reviewed: May 2021).

p 140   Lutteroth, J. (2012). Dreist, dreister, Deutschland. DER SPIEGEL. https://perma.cc/4TXE-6BDU (Page last reviewed: May 2021).

p 141   Fagan, C. (2011). Paris Syndrome: A First-Class Problem for a First-Class Vacation. The Atlantic. https://perma.cc/2MX8-UYHD (Page last reviewed: May 2021).

p 142   Andrews, E. (2020). The History of the Handshake. History.com. https://perma.cc/3AP7-C376 (Page last reviewed: May 2021).
         Walsh, C. (2020). Wither the handshake? The Harvard Gazette. https://perma.cc/5YBY-HANS (Page last reviewed: May 2021).

p 143   Fernau, L. (2019). Warum die Farbe Rosa einst Männersache war. GEO. https://perma.cc/9BL8-WW8L (Page last reviewed: May 2021).

p 144   Alle, K., & Mayerl, J. (2010). Der Bystander-Effekt in alltäglichen Hilfesituationen: Ein nicht-reaktives Feldexperiment. Schriftenreihe des Instituts für Sozialwissenschaften der Universität Stuttgart. https://perma.cc/ZT9K-JP5Y

p 145   Nunn, G. (2015). How to sneeze in Japanese. LOL (or, as they say in Indonesia, wkwkwk). The Guardian. https://perma.cc/A7ZA-GMKQ (Page last reviewed: May 2021).

p 146   Guttenberger, S. (2014). Wieso ist Gähnen ansteckend? Spektrum.de. https://perma.cc/MB3R-PX87 (Page last reviewed: May 2021).

p 147   Shapiro, M. (2019). Suicide Rates Spike in Spring, Not Winter. John Hopkins Medicine. https://perma.cc/C2PV-ZKCC (Page last reviewed: May 2021).

p 148   NASA (2020). Voyager. Jot Propulsion Laboratory California Institute of Technology. https://perma.cc/23Q3-R3A7 (Page last reviewed: May 2021).

p 149   Pinker, S. (2011). Gewalt: Eine neue Geschichte der Menschheit. S. Fischer.